PRAISE FOR *The Bedford Anthology*
of American Literature

"In a number of respects, this anthology is exceptional. *The Bedford Anthology* has two major advantages: a realistic balance of texts that acknowledges the frequent practice of assigning novels and autobiographies in full, and an incredibly fruitful, focused approach guided by questions of print culture and its attendant questions of authorship, circulation, and reception of literary texts."

— Matt Cohen
Duke University

"Unlike many other anthologies, I can see myself teaching almost everything included here. Not only is the anthology representative, but it also serves to focus on some of the chief issues in American studies today."

— Rosemary Fithian Guruswamy
Radford University

"Susan Belasco and Linck Johnson have done a fine job conceptualizing a kind of American literature anthology not currently available. Their focused attention to reading, writing, and print culture will remind students (and all of us) of the significance of literature as a way of knowing. As I read I also considered whether the introductory American survey I teach would need significant revision if I were to use an anthology like this one. I found I could teach *my* course with *their* book."

— Patti Cowell
Colorado State University

"I admire this anthology a great deal, but what recommends it, finally, is not simply its economies but the acuity of its choices, the unobtrusive depth of its learning, and its pedagogical and historical imaginativeness."

— Richard Millington
Smith College

"My overall reaction to this anthology is that it is one of the most thought-
fully organized and written anthologies of American literature that I have
seen in recent years. Rich in visual materials, which are especially effective
for an undergraduate audience, it is equally fulfilling in the content and
choice of selections."

— Sharon M. Harris
University of Connecticut

"In sum, this text offers the best view of the cultural mosaic that is 'American
Literature' that I have ever seen. I love the clear organization, and the various
helpful apparati, especially the historical contextualizations of a work's
particular 'place and time.'"

— Thomas Gannon
University of Nebraska

"Its selections are judiciously made, its introductions sound and focused on
the real-world concerns of authorship in American history, its contextual
material diverse, enriching, and to-the-point. I think that instructors who
want for their undergraduate students a manageable anthology with an
essential and diverse selection of texts, engaging biographical introductions,
and contexts that ground the literature practically in the world of reading,
publishing, and authorship will find *The Bedford Anthology of American
Literature* a very attractive choice."

— Robert D. Habich
Ball State University

"I know many American literature professors who have forsworn using
anthologies in the survey courses because of their unwieldiness, cost, and
symbolic 'comprehensiveness.' This volume rethinks the concept of
anthology. It takes a sophisticated, forward-looking curricular position and
invites us all to rethink how we introduce students to American literature."

— Susan Tomlinson
University of Massachusetts, Boston

"The introductions are acute and generous without being overwhelming; they
suggest depth without going into detail that might be stultifying to the new
student of American literature."

— Daniel Wardrop
Western Michigan State University

The Bedford Anthology
of American Literature

VOLUME TWO
1865 to the Present

Editorial Advisory Board, Volume Two

Elizabeth Ammons, *Tufts University*
Stephanie Browner, *Berea College*
Donna Campbell, *Washington State University*
David Chinitz, *Loyola University Chicago*
Michael Coyle, *Colgate University*
Robert Donahoo, *Sam Houston State University*
AnaLouise Keating, *Texas Woman's University*
Linda Morris, *University of California, Davis*
Paul Sorrentino, *Virginia Polytechnic Institute and State University*
Michael Soto, *Trinity University*
Nicholas Spencer, *University of Nebraska, Lincoln*
Susan Tomlinson, *University of Massachusetts, Boston*

The Bedford Anthology of American Literature

VOLUME TWO
1865 to the Present

Susan Belasco
University of Nebraska, Lincoln

Linck Johnson
Colgate University

Bedford / St. Martin's
BOSTON · NEW YORK

For Bedford / St. Martin's

EXECUTIVE EDITOR: Stephen A. Scipione
SENIOR DEVELOPMENTAL EDITOR: Maura Shea
SENIOR PRODUCTION EDITOR: Lori Chong Roncka
PRODUCTION SUPERVISOR: Jennifer Peterson
EXECUTIVE MARKETING MANAGER: Jenna Bookin Barry
MARKETING MANAGER: Adrienne Petsick
ASSOCIATE DEVELOPMENTAL EDITOR: Abby Bielagus
EDITORIAL ASSISTANT: Erin McGhee
PRODUCTION ASSISTANT: Lidia MacDonald-Carr
COPYEDITOR: Mary Lou Wilshaw-Watts
TEXT DESIGN: Judith Arisman, Arisman Design Studio
COVER DESIGN: Donna Lee Dennison
COVER ART: *Angel's Flight*, 1931, by Millard Sheets (32.17). Museum Associates /
    LACMA, Gift of Mrs. L. M. Maitland. Photo © Museum Associates / LACMA.
COMPOSITION: Stratford/TexTech
PRINTING AND BINDING: Quebecor World Taunton

PRESIDENT: Joan E. Feinberg
EDITORIAL DIRECTOR: Denise B. Wydra
EDITOR IN CHIEF: Karen S. Henry
DIRECTOR OF MARKETING: Karen Melton Soeltz
DIRECTOR OF EDITING, DESIGN, AND PRODUCTION: Marcia Cohen
MANAGING EDITOR: Elizabeth M. Schaaf

Library of Congress Control Number: 2006921308

Copyright © 2008 by Bedford / St. Martin's

All rights reserved. No part of this book may be reproduced, stored in a retrieval
system, or transmitted in any form or by any means, electronic, mechanical,
photocopying, recording, or otherwise, except as may be expressly permitted by
the applicable copyright statutes or in writing by the Publisher.

Manufactured in the United States of America.

2 1 0 9 8
f e d c b

For information, write: Bedford / St. Martin's, 75 Arlington Street, Boston, MA
02116 (617-399-4000)

ISBN-10: 0-312-41208-8 (Volume Two)
ISBN-13: 978-0-312-41208-1

ISBN-10: 0-312-48299-X (Volume One)
ISBN-13: 978-0-312-48299-2

*Acknowledgments and copyrights appear at the back of the book on pages
1554-64, which constitutes an extension of the copyright page. It is a violation of
the law to reproduce these selections by any means whatsoever without the
written permission of the copyright holder.*

For Max Johnson and Stephen Jenkins

Preface

The Bedford Anthology of American Literature is designed to meet the challenge of teaching courses that cover American literature from its beginnings to the present day. That challenge has grown even more daunting during the last three decades, as the canon has expanded dramatically. We have been studying, teaching, and writing about American literature for over thirty years, yet like all teachers we grapple with questions about the selection, organization, and presentation of material, especially in relation to a changing student population. Indeed, even as instructors have recognized the claims of a growing number of writers and kinds of writings for a place on our syllabi, college students have become increasingly diverse in their backgrounds, experiences, and ration for literary study. At the same time, rapid changes in technology have shaped students' understanding of language and communication, as ear-sponses to both texts and textbooks.

The Bedford Anthology of American Literature takes a new ap American literature. The editors of any anthology inevitabl lier editors, and we have learned much from our pred anthologies of American literature become thicker volumes, however, we are concerned by the im and students alike. How, in the limited spa hope to cover the ever-growing list of small number of the selections in mos they find themselves skipping over large portions of an expensive anthology? Moreover, although we are deeply committed to anthologies as the most effective medium for representing the full range of American literature, we know from direct experience and the comments of other instructors that students find it awkward and unappealing to read certain kinds of works, especially novels and other extended prose narratives, in the somewhat cumbersome format of an anthology.

The Bedford Anthology of American Literature represents an effort to preserve the strengths of traditional anthologies while responding to changes in both the canon and in teaching methods that have emerged during the last thirty years. At every stage of our work on this anthology, we have been guided by the needs of instructors and their students. We have drawn on our extensive experiences at a wide range of institutions, and we have communicated with hundreds of instructors in colleges and universities across the country about how a new anthology might best meet their needs and the needs of contemporary college students. While the texts, notes, and introductions are based on current scholarship in the field, to which we are deeply indebted, *The Bedford Anthology of American Literature* is a tool for teaching and learning, and it aims at broad representation rather than comprehensive coverage. It consequently provides a rich but not unlimited range of choices to instructors facing the daunting task of creating syllabi and reading assignments of representative works from every period of American literature.

Two of the major pedagogical challenges facing teachers of the American literature survey course are engaging students in the readings and helping them understand history and context. We have, therefore, sought to bring together in an attractive format texts chosen on the basis of their literary or historical importance, their inherent interest, and their proven effectiveness in the classroom, either when studied on their own or in relation to other texts in the anthology. In addition to a core of commonly taught texts that instructors rely on, we have included rarely anthologized texts that have proven to be very successful in the classroom. We have also given some prominence to various kinds of life writings, which we view as a vital element in American literature and which we have found to be particularly attractive to students. In a further effort to stimulate student interest in and understanding of literary texts, as well as of their vital social, political, and cultural contexts, we have also incorporated features, including illustrations, that show the changing material conditions in which literary works were ...duced. We have thus sought to offer in reasonably compact volumes a foundation of ...tial texts that instructors need with a substantial amount of additional material ...them construct their own surveys of American literature. For students, our ...ffers a variety of ways to read and think about American literature and, we ... greater understanding and appreciation of it.

A ... of *The Bedford Anthology of American Literature,*
Volumes One and Two

...iterary Works.   The selection of writers and works has ...tandings of and approaches to American literature that ...ee decades. The selections consequently reflect the rich diversity of American literature, especially in terms of gender, race, and ethnicity. At the same time, the selection of writers and texts has been guided by what is actually taught in survey courses of American literature, based on extensive analysis of syllabi and reviews by over five hundred instructors nationwide.

An Apparatus Designed and Written for Students.   We have sought to make the introductory materials in the anthology lively and readable, while providing other features designed to engage the interest of students and enhance their appreciation and understanding of the texts. Biographical introductions highlight important aspects of the authors' backgrounds and experiences, while charting the course of their careers as writers. Marginal quotations, most often an appreciative observation by another writer, call attention to the characteristics or value of the author's work, and Web site references point to further information. Individual prose works and groups of poems are separately introduced in a selection headnote that provides information about the writing and publication of the works, as well as brief comments on their distinctive features or literary and historical significance. Explanatory notes are provided for each text and are designed to foster reading comprehension and assist students in understanding a work, not to provide critical commentary on the text. Indeed, we have consistently sought to provide contexts for reading texts and to raise questions designed to stimulate discussion rather than to offer interpretations of the texts.

Abraham Cahan
[1860–1951]

Abraham Cahan
This photograph was taken when Cahan was twenty-three, about two years after his arrival in New York City.

Abraham Cahan was born on July 7, 1860, in Podberezy, a shtetl or Jewish community in Russia. His parents were Sarah and Shakne Cahan, a teacher at a Hebrew school. When Cahan was about five years old, the family moved a short distance away to the larger city of Vilna. Both Podberezy and Vilna were situated in the Pale of Jewish Settlement, the area in eastern Russia where all Jews were required by law to live. The language spoken in the shtetl was Yiddish, a dialect combining words from Hebrew and several European languages, especially German. From an early age, Cahan developed a deep understanding of the value and importance of language through his intensive study of Hebrew, the Jewish Bible, and the Talmud, the body of Jewish civil and ceremonial law and legend. But he later decided to pursue secular studies at the Vilna Teacher Training Institute for Jewish students, which he attended from 1876 to 1881. While there, he was drawn to the revolutionary politics and socialism of students who opposed the political autocracy of Russia. The assassination of Czar Alexander II in 1881 prompted a wave of repression and violence directed against Russian Jews. Cahan, who had secured a job teaching in a school at Velizh, came under suspicion for possessing radical publications. Certain that he would be arrested and probably executed, Cahan fled Russia, joining more than 13,000 other Jews who left the country in 1882.

After a long and dangerous journey across Europe to England, Cahan booked a passage in steerage from Liverpool to New York City. During the voyage, he began to study English with the help of a Russian-English dictionary and a sailor who knew a few Russian words. Admitted through Ellis Island into the United States on June 7, 1882, Cahan joined thousands of other Jewish immigrants who had settled on the Lower East Side of Manhattan, then known as the "Ghetto." Even as he undertook the difficult task of earning a living in the overcrowded, impoverished section of the city, Cahan set about learning English. By the next year, his language skills were sufficient for him to begin teaching English to immigrants at the Young Men's Hebrew Association. In 1885, he met and married Aniuta (Anna) Bronstein, an immigrant from Kiev, Russia. Increasingly active in city politics and organized labor, Cahan formally joined the Socialist Labor Party in 1887. He soon began lecturing and writing articles in English on Jewish life in the city for several newspapers in New York. Revising a lecture he had delivered at the New York Labor Lyceum, Cahan also published "Realism," which appeared in the *Workman's Advocate* in 1889. As he later described it in his autobiography, the essay was "a philosophic consideration of the nature of art," based on his study of contemporary art and his reading of William Dean Howells, Henry James, and the Russian novelist Leo Tolstoy. Naturalized as an American citizen on June 8, 1891, Cahan continued to write articles in both English and Yiddish and edited a socialist newspaper published in Yiddish, the *Arbeter Tsaytung*, or "Worker's Journal."

He also began to write fiction. Cahan's first short story in English, "A Providential Match," appeared in *Short Stories* in 1895, the same year he published a serialized novel in Yiddish in the *Arbeter Tsaytung*. His efforts were strongly encouraged by William Dean Howells, who in 1895 told Cahan, "It is your duty to write." Buoyed by the support of an American writer he greatly admired, Cahan translated and published his serialized novel as *Yekl: A Tale of the New York Ghetto* (1896), which Howells enthusiastically reviewed in the *New York World*. "Suddenly I was known in American literature," Cahan later recalled. But he could not support himself and his family through literature alone. In 1897, he helped establish what would become the leading Yiddish newspaper in the world, the *Jewish Daily Forward*. Cahan subsequently edited the newspaper for a total of fifty years. But he also continued to write in English for other New York newspapers and to publish articles and stories in magazines, including the prestigious *Atlantic Monthly*. A collection of five of his stories, *The Imported Bridegroom and Other Stories of the New York Ghetto*, was published in 1898. In a review of the volume, Howells once again praised Cahan's realism, observing that "the author handles [his materials] so skillfully that he holds the reader between a laugh and a heartache, and fashions into figures so lifelike that you would expect to meet them in any stroll through Hester-street," the busy artery at the heart of the Jewish community in New York City.

From that point on, Cahan was a prominent writer in both English and Yiddish. As the editor of the *Forward*, he was known for his articles on social reform and labor policy. Although he published a second novel in English, *The White Terror and the Red: A Novel of Revolutionary Russia* (1905), Cahan increasingly wanted to concentrate on journalism. At the invitation of the editors of *McClure's Magazine*, however, he wrote an extended fictional piece loosely based on some of the events of his life, *The Autobiography of an American Jew: The Rise of David Levinsky*, which was serialized in the magazine from April through July 1913. In revised form, Cahan later published it as *The Rise of David Levinsky: A Novel* (1917), now widely regarded as one of the most important works of early Jewish American fiction. During the same period, he began to write his actual autobiography, *The Education of Abraham Cahan*, which was published in five volumes between 1926 and 1936. Cahan continued to devote his energies to the *Forward*, serving as a spokesperson for American Jews and, after two visits to Palestine, becoming active in the Zionist movement. He also had the satisfaction of seeing many of his early fictional works reprinted in new editions. "Socialist leader, novelist, critic, and newspaper man," as he was described in the obituary in the *New York Times*, Cahan died on August 31, 1951.

[Cahan] sees his people humorously, and he is as unsparing of their sordidness as he is compassionate of their hard circumstance and the somewhat frowsy pathos of their lives.
—William Dean Howells

bedfordstmartins.com/ americanlit for research links on Cahan

Cahan's "A Ghetto Wedding." This story was first published in the *Atlantic Monthly* only two months before it appeared in Cahan's collection *The Imported Bridegroom and Other Stories of the New York Ghetto* (1898).

An Emphasis on Complete Works.   In choosing selections for the anthology, we have sought to include complete texts – rather than excerpts – whenever possible. In Volume Two, we have included portions of extended works of nonfiction that can be effectively excerpted, including Sarah Winnemucca Hopkins's *Life among the Piutes*, Booker T. Washington's *Up from Slavery*, and W. E. B. Du Bois's *The Souls of Black Folk*. But all poems are printed in their entirety, and we have selected sketches, stories, or novellas rather than excerpts from novels. Lengthy works of fiction, which we believe students find far more comfortable to read as separate texts, are not included in the anthology. While we hope that many instructors will find the selections from key writers fully adequate for their purposes, we understand that other instructors may well wish to supplement the anthology with longer works of fiction. In order to make such works available for packaging with the anthology or for independent purchase, Bedford / St. Martin's has published the Bedford College Editions, attractive (and very competitively priced) reprints of five of the most frequently taught American novels: Nathaniel Hawthorne's *The Scarlet Letter*, Harriet Beecher Stowe's *Uncle Tom's Cabin*, Herman Melville's *Benito Cereno*, Mark Twain's *Adventures of Huckleberry Finn*, and Kate Chopin's *The Awakening*.

An Organization Designed for Greater Coherence and Comprehension.   The overall organization of the anthology is chronological. Volume One begins with Native American origin tales and concludes with the Civil War. Volume Two covers writers from 1865 to the present. Each volume, in turn, is divided into three **literary periods**. Within each of those periods, we have divided selections into related groups of authors or kinds of texts. Such **chapter groupings** are designed to serve several purposes. First, they bring into close proximity within the anthology works that might naturally be taught together, thus creating fruitful juxtapositions and helping instructors create coherent syllabi. We have also sought to address a problem we have often encountered when teaching with anthologies. Students sometimes find it difficult to relate the general information provided in a period introduction to the specific selections that follow or tend to forget much of that information by the time they read selections toward the end of the period. In addition to an introduction to each period, we also offer an introduction to each group of selections within the period, focusing on the specific cultural, historical, and especially literary backgrounds students may need in order to read those selections with understanding and appreciation.

A Unifying Theme on the History of Reading and Writing in America Provides Contexts for the Literature.   A thematic thread – the history of reading and writing in America – is woven throughout both volumes to assist students in understanding the context of the works and to emphasize the role literature has played in the unfolding story of culture and history in what became the United States. In the period introductions, as well as in the introductions to groups of authors and texts within each period, we emphasize developments such as the growth of literacy, the expansion of the educational system, changes in the production and distribution of books, and the emergence and increasing importance of periodicals in the literary culture of the United States. We further develop that theme in our introductions to authors, in which we indicate the ways such developments shaped their writings and literary careers, as well as in our

American Literature
1914–1945

◄ The Wharf Theatre

In the summer of 1916, the Provincetown Players gave their first public perfor-
mances in a converted, 25 × 35 foot fishing shack at the end of Lewis Wharf in
Provincetown, Massachusetts. Members of the group rigged up rudimentary
lighting, created benches by resting planks on sawhorses, and built a 10 × 12 foot
stage in the ramshackle building, which many theater historians view as the
birthplace of modern American drama.

The Emergence
of Modern American Drama

DURING THE EARLY DECADES of the twentieth century, "Broadway," the
area around Times Square in New York City, at once symbolized and domi-
nated theater in the United States. Many of the plays performed by hundreds of touring companies originated on Broadway, where the number of
theatrical productions rose from seventy during the 1900–01 season to a
peak of almost three hundred during 1926–27, after which the audience for
theater was eroded by the growing popularity of "talkies" in the movies
and the onset of the Great Depression. Operettas were especially popular
on Broadway, as were musical extravaganzas such as Florenz Ziegfeld's
Follies, which he produced virtually every year from 1907 through 1927.

773

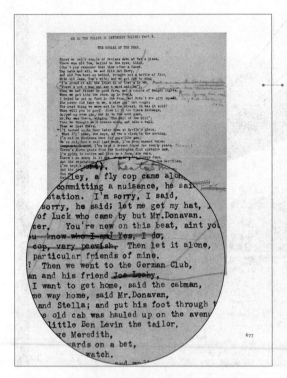

headnotes to selections, in which we discuss the writing and initial publication of the works. The history of reading and writing is further delineated in illustrations ranging from **manuscript pages**, including the opening page to T. S. Eliot's original typescript version of *The Waste Land* through a wide array of printed materials, such as the frontispiece to the original 1912 edition of Mary Antin's *The Promised Land.*

"American Contexts" Highlight a Wide Range of Writings under Compelling Topics.   In addition to the works of the individual authors included in the anthology, briefer selections from many other writers are gathered together in clusters of related works called "**American Contexts.**" Those sections focus on topics ranging from "Colonial Diaries and Journals" to "'Mine Eyes Have Seen the Glory': The Meanings of the Civil War" in Volume One and, in Volume Two, from "'The America of the Mind': Critics, Writers, and the Representation of Reality" to "'Inventing the Truth': The Contemporary Memoir." Such clusters are designed to extend the range and resonance of the anthology by introducing additional voices and other kinds of writing, from diaries, journals, and memoirs to editorials, critical essays, political speeches, and social criticism. Although individual selections within those clusters could of course be assigned separately, the "American Contexts" are designed as coherent units, most often intended to be taught as either an introduction or a coda to a larger period or grouping in the anthology. Some clusters invite discussion of distinctive genres, while others allow an opportunity to explore contested ideological issues, critical controversies, cultural developments, and responses to events such as the Civil War.

"Through a Modern Lens" Helps Students Make Connections between Writers from the Past and the Present.   In order to bring later perspectives to bear on some of the writers and texts in Volume One, we have included brief sections throughout the volume under the general rubric "**Through a Modern Lens.**" These include but are not limited to N. Scott Momaday's recent celebration of Native American origin and creation stories, Robert Lowell's exploration of one of the most prominent eighteenth-century writers in "Mr. Edwards and the Spider," and a tribute by the contemporary African American poet Kevin Young to Phillis Wheatley. In addition to revealing connections across time and space, the "Through a Modern Lens" feature offers rich opportunities for discussion of a number of connected issues: the imaginative effort required to understand the attitudes, conditions, and modes of expression of earlier periods; the sometimes tense rela-

American Contexts

"MAKE IT NEW":
POETS ON POETRY

IN HIS TRANSLATION OF THE *TA HIO* ("The Great Learning") of the ancient Chinese philosopher Confucius, the influential modern poet and critic Ezra Pound reaffirmed, "Renew thyself daily, utterly, make it new, and again new, make it new." The exhortation "make it new," a phrase that Pound later used as the title of a collection of his essays, consequently became a kind of shorthand for the complex and often conflicting agendas of American poets during the early decades of the twentieth century.

As the following commentaries by poets suggest, there was considerable disagreement among them about the ways in which poetry could be made new and what constituted the new poetry. In her introductory essay in the first issue of *Poetry: A Magazine of Verse* in 1912, its founder and editor Harriet Monroe affirmed that "all forms, whether narrative, dramatic, or lyric, will be acceptable." Monroe subsequently published a wide range of poetry in her magazine, which strongly encouraged both established and emerging poets in the United States. During the decades following the founding of *Poetry*, however, all of the elements of poetry — form, language, rhythm, rhyme, and subject matter — were topics of serious discussion and debate. Divisions emerged even within the first organized group of modern poets writing in English, the imagistes or imagists. Pound, the first leader of the group, described their fundamental aesthetic values and

538

---

poetic techniques in an essay published in *Poetry* in 1913. But he soon came into conflict with Amy Lowell, who was determined to democratize what Pound, using the French term, called imagisme and she called imagism, primarily in an effort to make such modern poetry seem less foreign or alien to audiences in the United States. As Lowell embarked on a crusade for imagism in essays such as "The New Manner in Modern Poetry," Pound moved in other directions, working with other new poets such as T. S. Eliot. In his 1919 essay "Tradition and the Individual Talent," Eliot challenged poets and critics who rejected "tradition" by emphasizing the vital connections between modern poets and poets of the past, a European tradition extending back to the ancient Greek poet Homer.

MAKE IT NEW
ESSAYS BY
EZRA POUND

新
日
新

LONDON
FABER AND FABER LIMITED
24 RUSSELL SQUARE

*Ezra Pound,
Make It New*
The title of this 1934 collection of essays is Pound's translation of the four Chinese characters on the title page, which may more literally be translated "make new, day by day, make new."

During the period from the 1920s through World War II, many poets grappled with questions about the function and status of poetry in the modern age. For poets of the Harlem Renaissance, questions about the language, sources, and subject matter of poetry were central to the contested issue of whether there was or could be what Langston Hughes described as "any true Negro Art in America." James Weldon Johnson rejected the tradition of dialect poetry, which he argued was not "capable of giving expression to the varied conditions of Negro life in America." Hughes, who frequently wrote in dialect, encouraged African American poets to produce work that was racial in both subject and treatment, drawing inspiration from indigenous traditions of music such as spirituals and jazz. In her essay "Modern Poetry," the poet and painter Mina Loy also emphasized the close relations between poetry and music, as well as the vital connections between "the renaissance in poetry" and the "composite language" forged by members of various races and immigrant groups in the United States. Hart Crane suggested that urban life and technological advances opened new subjects for poets, exploring what in his 1930 essay "Modern Poetry" he described as the "function of poetry in a Machine Age." The poet most closely associated with rural New England, Robert Frost, reaffirmed some of the traditional forms and functions of poetry in "The Figure a Poem Makes" (1939), published near the end of the Great Depression. During that period of economic crisis, many viewed modern poetry as immaterial, and it was

bedfordstmartins.com/ americanlit for research links on the authors in this section

---

Occom through a Modern Lens

IN THE LATE EIGHTEENTH CENTURY, works by Native Americans who wrote in English were published by several printers, including Thomas and Samuel Green, descendants of a prominent family of colonial printers. The Greens printed dozens of sermons and religious books on their press in New London, Connecticut. They published Samson Occom's collection of hymns and spiritual songs, as well as his sermon on the execution of Moses Paul. Occom's works went through several editions during the eighteenth century and enjoyed considerable popularity. But Occom's autobiographical sketch existed only in manuscript until it was finally published in 1982. Since then, he has been the object of considerable attention by scholars, including James Ottery, a professor of English, a member of the Brothertown Indian Nation, and a descendant of Occom, whose name he spells Occum. Ottery wrote the following poem as he was contemplating the "silences" in Occom's "Diary," which he kept over many years and in which he wrote *A Short Narrative of My Life*. Some commentators have stressed Occom's failure to mention some of the devastating events of his life in his narrative, while scholars have emphasized its limitations as a source of ethnographic information about Native Americans. In contrast, Ottery meditates on the obstacles that confronted a Native American attempting to put his "life into words in the language / that wasn't his mother tongue." The text, which incorporates Occom's words, is taken from the online publication of the poem (http://work.colum.edu/~jottery/IntroCW/NAC/SamsonOccum.htm).

The Reverend Mr. Samson Occom
This portrait of Occom, described in an accompanying caption as the "first Indian Minister that ever was in Europe," was published in London during or shortly after his triumphant fund-raising tour of England. Occom wrote his brief narrative of his life soon after his return to America.

410

James Ottery
[b. 1953]

THE DIARY OF SAMSON OCCUM

He put his life into words: his life
as a Presbyterian preacher,[1] his life
as a preacher and teacher before that
in the Society for Propagating the Gospel in New England,
two years of his life spent raising   5
money in old England for the Indian Charity School
in Connecticut, "funds misdirected"
for the founding of a white Dartmouth College instead.
He put his life into words, in the language
that was not his mother tongue, the language   10
not learned until he was 16;
in the language that was not his
until he reached the age of 16,
he wrote of his life until then in very few words
of the language that wasn't his mother tongue —   15

    *I was born a Heathen
    and Brought up in Heathenism
    until I was between 16 & 17 Years of age,
    at a place call'd Mohegan . . .*[2]

He put his life into words in the language   20
that wasn't his mother tongue, the English learned
first when he was 16,
(he would begin reading Hebrew at 21,
until "after a year of study" he would stop,
because "his eyes would fail him"),   25
In the language that was not his mother tongue
he would write:

    *Having Seen and heard Several Representations,
    In England and Scotland [two words crossed out]*

---

1. **Presbyterian preacher:** Occom was ordained a Presbyterian minister in 1759.
2. *I . . . Mohegan:* The opening lines of Occom's narrative.

411

tions between later readers and writers and earlier texts; and the ongoing influence of earlier authors on writers in the twentieth and twenty-first centuries, even as the works of those later writers reveal markedly different aesthetic values, literary practices, and philosophical or religious convictions.

Appealing Two-Color Design and Extensive Illustration Program Make Literature Inviting and Accessible for Today's Readers.   Each volume in *The Bedford Anthology of American Literature* includes more than two hundred carefully selected illustrations, ranging from engravings published in early travel narratives and examples of Native American arts to portraits of writers, paintings or photographs of contemporary scenes, and a wide range of images illustrating the history of literary and print culture, including manuscript pages, broadsides, periodicals, and the covers, frontispieces, and title pages of books. Although their inclusion is in part designed to enhance the attractiveness of and the experience of reading selections in the volumes, the primary purpose of the illustrations is pedagogical. Through our own teaching and in discussions with many other instructors, we have discovered that students increasingly respond to such visual materials, especially those that help them connect with authors and grasp the cultural, material, and social conditions in which literary works were produced. In fact, many of the selections in both volumes of this anthology were first published in illustrated books or periodicals, and such illustrations can generate fruitful discussions about both the literary work and its initial audience. In various ways, those and other illustrations raise questions about identity – the role of class, gender, race, and religion – and about self-representation and the representation of reality, questions that we believe may offer useful points of departure for a discussion of the central concerns and broader contexts of the literary texts. Thumbnails of some of the illustrations are used as visual markers in the timelines, which along with several maps are designed to help students negotiate the long history and the complex geography covered in *The Bedford Anthology of American Literature*.

A Note on Editorial Procedures

In general, we have taken the texts in the anthology from the first printings or from authoritative modern editions of early books and manuscripts. As far as is practicable, we have sought to reproduce the texts as they were originally written or published, retaining their historical features in order to preserve the flavor of the authors' styles and familiarize students with changes in English usage and the conventions of capitalization, punctuation, and spelling. Since spelling was not standardized until the late eighteenth century, we do not alter British spellings, such as *humour*; early variant spellings that can be clearly understood, such as *chearful* for *cheerful*; early past tense forms, such as *learnt* for *learned*; or contractions that were commonly used in early texts, such as *us'd* for *used* and *tho'* for *though*. To aid students in their reading of early texts, we have provided footnotes for many terms that are now archaic or obsolete. We have altered early printer's conventions that would cause confusion, such as the long *s* in *Bleſſings*, which is printed as *Blessings*. We have silently expanded some abbreviations,